THE
POCKET

GOOD
LUCK

Published in 2024
by Gemini Adult Books Ltd
Part of Gemini Books Group

Based in Woodbridge and London

Marine House, Tide Mill Way
Woodbridge, Suffolk IP12 1AP
United Kingdom
www.geminibooks.com

Text and Design © 2024 Gemini Adult Books Ltd
Part of the Gemini Pockets series

Cover image: travel images/Alamy Stock Photo

ISBN 978 1 80247 267 7

A CIP catalogue record for this book is available from the British Library.

Printed in China

10 9 8 7 6 5 4 3 2 1

Images: Adobe Stock: 6, 18, 26, 42, 50, 54, 62, 70, 74, 86, 98, 106, 118.
Freepix: 10, 30, 34, 82. Shutterstock: 14 Elena LAtkun, 38, 110 Albinaster,
46 PixelSquid3d, 58 Lena Solodovnikova, 66 Alex Desing, 78 brandianna_
art, 90 Marish, 94 Lerha, 102 Kobrynska,114 Luis Bruno, 122 MoreMass,
126 Karla Leon. Wikicommons: 22 Assafn

THE POCKET

GOOD LUCK

30 charms to
bring fortune
your way

Introduction

As long as there have been human beings on the planet, they have turned to objects and symbols to bring them luck and protect them from evil. These good luck charms, talismans and amulets brought comfort to their owners in hard times and spread positivity and optimism, and still do today.

Some good luck symbols remain specific to a certain region or country, while others travelled as people migrated around the world, evolving and blending with new cultures along the way. With origins deeply rooted in folk tales, myths and religious practices, the stories of these charms are fascinating and diverse.

Read on to Get Lucky!

"Luck affects everything; let your hook be always cast; In the stream where you least expect it, there will be a fish."

Ovid, *Heroides*

Acorn

PLACE OF ORIGIN:
England/Scandinavia (Norse myths)

KEY TRAITS:
Strength, Protection, Healing, Youth,
Prosperity, Fertility, Rebirth

The distinctive fruit of the mighty oak, acorns have been known for their talismanic properties since ancient times, when the Greeks and Romans associated oaks with their most powerful deities and with great fortitude and strength. The Norse god of thunder and lightning, Thor, is also linked to the oak, which both attracts lightning and withstands powerful storms. As a result, the acorn has long been seen as a protective charm in Nordic cultures.

Symbolic of new beginnings, health and vitality, carrying or wearing an acorn on a necklace is believed to bring luck, protect against sickness and pain, and to accelerate healing. In England, where the oak is the national tree, wearing an acorn around the neck was said to ward off premature ageing.

* An acorn placed on a windowsill will bring good luck to a home and protects it from storms, lightning and danger. Acorn motifs on furniture and other interior decoration echo this belief today.

* During the Norman Conquest, English soldiers carried acorns in their pockets for protection during battle and as a symbol of English pride and strength.

* Acorns were used by druids and witches to identify one another. When passing on a path, they would hand one another acorns to let them know who they were and that they were in good company.

"Accumulating love brings luck, accumulating hatred brings calamity. Anyone who fails to recognize problems leaves the door open for tragedies to rush in."

Paulo Coelho, *Warrior of the Light*

Carp

PLACE OF ORIGIN:
Eastern Europe, China and Japan

KEY TRAITS:
Good fortune, Abundance, Perseverance,
Strength, Fertility

The freshwater carp is a traditional Christmas Eve meal in Eastern Europe, particularly Poland, Slovakia and the Czech Republic, where its scales are kept throughout the year as lucky charms. Since the 12th century, carp have been a prized dish, fit for nobles and kings, and it's from this time that the custom arose of keeping a carp scale in the wallet to attract wealth in the coming year.

Japanese legend states that a group of koi carp swimming up a river came across a waterfall and, after one hundred years of jumping, finally reached the top. Ever since, the fish has symbolized perseverance and courage in Japan. In China, the image of the carp jumping a waterfall signifies success, while two carp swimming together embody fertility and harmony.

* When preparing carp for the Christmas Eve meal, the scales – which look a little like coins – are removed and dried. One is placed under each plate at the table for guests to keep in their wallets until the following year.

* Eating carp as part of the Chinese New Year festivities is believed to attract good luck and gifts because the Chinese characters for these words are similar to those in the word "carp".

* May 5th is Children's Day in Japan and every year families fly *koinobori* – brightly coloured streamers in the shape of carp – outside their homes to celebrate and encourage the koi's characteristics of bravery and perseverance.

One Polish tradition was to buy a Christmas Eve carp live from the market and keep it swimming in the bathtub for a couple of days before it became the holiday meal.

Chimney Sweep

COUNTRY OF ORIGIN:
England

KEY TRAITS:
Luck, Marital harmony, Fertility

With their classic all-black uniform, dusty faces and distinctive brushes, chimney sweeps have been considered lucky for hundreds of years. Their status as a lucky symbol originates from the time a sweep is said to have saved the life of King George II by grabbing the reins of his horse when it bolted during a procession. The king issued a royal decree declaring that sweeps brought good luck and should always be treated with the greatest respect.

Sweeps were also accorded the right to wear top hat and tails – something usually reserved for the gentry – and soon became a popular addition to a wedding party, bestowing their luck on the marriage of the bride and groom. This tradition continues today and chimney sweeps are hired to attend weddings to give the groom a lucky handshake and the bride a lucky kiss.

* Make a wish if you are lucky enough to see a chimney sweep's brush poking out of the top of a chimney.

* In Germany, Austria and Hungary, it's especially lucky to see a chimney sweep on New Year's Day and sweeps are often depicted on New Year's cards and postcards exchanged to offer friends and relatives luck for the coming year.

* When the Duke of Edinburgh married the future Queen Elizabeth II in 1947, he was given a "Lucky Send-off" by the palace chimney sweep when he left Kensington Palace for Westminster Abbey on his wedding day.

BAD LUCK!

Shoes on a Table

This common superstition that means you are "tempting fate" is particularly prevalent in Northern England, and has its roots in the coal mining industry. When a miner died in an accident, their shoes were placed on a table as a sign of respect. In the world of theatre, some believe that putting costume shoes on a table can foretell a future bad performance with the character the shoes belong to.

BAD LUCK!

Chinese
Red Knot

COUNTRY OF ORIGIN:
China

KEY TRAITS:
Luck, Love, Prosperity, Protection

Made from a single length of cord woven into different shapes, Chinese knots have been produced as folk art for millennia, acting as talismans to bring luck, ward off evil spirits and attract love and wealth. Usually satin, they are intricate, symmetrical and most commonly seen with tassels hanging underneath.

It's thought they were once crafted to record important information in times when few could write, but their symbolic associations with luck have grown over time. There are many different styles of knot, with some of the most common including the clover knot, for luck, the double coin knot, representing love and the circle of life, and the Pan Chang or "endless" knot, which represents the Buddhist principle of life without beginning or end and is believed to bring wealth.

* Also known as the mystic knot, the Chinese knot is believed to impart good fortune to those who wear it as an amulet or as decoration on their clothes.

* Chinese knots are most often red, the luckiest shade in Chinese culture; they can be found adorned with beads, charms and sometimes pieces of jade.

* Hold or rub the knot to drive away anxiety and anger and bring stability and tranquillity to the mind.

* Display the knot in your interior decoration where, according to the the principles of feng shui, it will increase the harmonious flow of chi energy in the home.

* Wear the knot on your right hand if you wish to boost your yang energy or on the left hand to activate yin energy.

An image of a double coin
knot was found on a banner
in a 2,000-year-old Chinese
tomb, which also showed two
deities linked to marriage,
hence the knot's association
with love. It is customary in
traditional Chinese wedding
ceremonies for the bride and
groom to each hold an end
of a concentric knot to bring
luck and bless the marriage.

Cornicello

COUNTRY OF ORIGIN:
Italy

KEY TRAITS:
Protection, Luck in relationships,
Fertility, Virility, Strength

In use since ancient times, the cornicello ("little horn") is a twisted, horn-shaped charm worn to repel the evil eye and to stimulate fertility. It especially guards against interference in the areas of marriage and relationships. Still a common good luck symbol in parts of Italy, it may have been inspired by the horn of the African eland antelope. Today the charm, which is commonly worn as a necklace, is often made from red coral to symbolize blood and looks more like a chilli pepper.

The cornicello is also connected to the cornucopia from Greek and Roman mythology. This "horn of plenty", created when Zeus broke a goat's horn, which was then permanently filled with food, is symbolic of fertility and abundance. Cornicelli are also linked to the male fertility god, Priapus, and sometimes worn by men as an amulet to protect their virility.

* Hang cornicelli outside a front door, or above a doorway or outside window, to protect everyone inside and grant them strength and fertility.

* Pregnant women and nursing mothers wear a cornicello to protect their children from the curses of the evil eye and so ensure the success of the next generation.

* A cornicello can be hung from a car's rear-view mirror to protect the vehicle and its inhabitants from harm. This is a custom that was first used on journeys to shield horses and mules from the evil eye and maleficence of strangers.

According to legend,
a cornicello should
be bought for you in
order to bring good
luck. If you buy it for
yourself, never pay
for the whole thing.

Dala Horse

COUNTRY OF ORIGIN:
Sweden

KEY TRAITS:
Dignity, Strength, Courage, Luck

The carved, painted Dala horse – or Dalahäst – originates from the Dalarna region in central Sweden and has become one of the country's most popular good luck symbols. The distinctive wooden horse with its colourful folk-art decoration is said to originate from 1716 when soldiers fighting for King Charles XII were billeted in Dalarna. During long winter evenings they carved wooden toys, most notably horses, which were especially revered. The carvings were traditionally given as gifts for hosts or as payment for food or room and board.

The stylized design of the horse today is around 150 years old, but the mass appeal of Dala horses really took off after the 1939 World's Fair in New York where a giant version featured in the Swedish pavilion, cementing its status as a national symbol. Usually red, they are sometimes found in other colours, each of which emphasize one of their auspicious traits.

* Dala horses bring luck wherever you place them in your home, but if you want to ward off evil, stand the horse with its hind legs towards the door, ready to kick bad spirits out if they come calling.

* Do as the Swedish do, and give a Dala horse at a major life event, such as a birth, wedding, anniversary or graduation.

* If you want to change the direction of your life, change the direction of your Dala horse to turn your fortunes around.

Representing power, wealth
and fertility, the horse was
worshipped as sacred by
pagan cults, associated with
the gods Freyr and Odin,
and essential to life for the
farmer and soldier. Wooden
horses have been found in
Viking graves, and whether
a toy or religious icon, the
Dala horse is a link back to
ancient beliefs.

Dragon

COUNTRY OF ORIGIN:
China

KEY TRAITS:
Luck, Strength, Health

Considered by many to be the most auspicious sign of the Chinese zodiac, dragons have long represented luck, strength and health in Chinese culture. Usually depicted as a snake-like creature with four legs, the dragon is a spiritual and cultural symbol denoting power, confidence and determination. It is also a rain deity that controls weather and fosters harmony.

In the Chinese creation myth, dragons are said to have aided the creator of all things in making the world, and there have been representations of them found in China since Neolithic times. Chinese emperors believed they were descendants of dragons, and dragon imagery has adorned imperial robes for more than 2,000 years. Today, they feature in many celebrations, including the annual dragon boat races and the dragon dances performed by Chinese communities worldwide at New Year.

* Dragon figures bring good fortune and protection in the home, especially when positioned near a source of water. Ensure, however, that they stand behind you in an office, to support you, rather than in front of you – as you might then find yourself in opposition to their forces.

* Liu Bang, founder of the Han dynasty, which ruled China for 400 years from 202 BCE, said he was conceived after his mother dreamt of a dragon, forever after linking the beasts with imperial power.

* Dragon colours hold significance with red symbolizing luck and prosperity, yellow indicating nobility and blue and green being associated with water and nature.

The dragon is the only
mythical creature in the
Chinese zodiac and more
babies are born in the year
of the dragon – every 12
years – than any other.
Those lucky enough to
be born under this sign
are known to be clever
and charming, optimistic,
strong and healthy.

Dreamcatcher

PLACE OF ORIGIN:
North America

KEY TRAITS:
Protection, Peaceful sleep

A woven web on a willow hoop, decorated with beads and hanging feathers, a dreamcatcher is a protective charm traditionally placed over cradles or beds in many Native American communities. They are associated with the legend of Asibikaashi, the Spider Woman, who catches bad dreams in her web, shielding sleeping children and adults from harm. Good dreams and good luck are able to pass through a dreamcatcher, while bad dreams and their associated negative energy dissipate by morning.

Dreams hold deep significance to the native cultures most closely associated with dream-catchers. The Ojibwe believe dreams can contain messages of guidance from the spirit world, for the self or the wider community. As such, dreamcatchers are sacred objects only to be used with the utmost reverence and respect for their indigenous origins.

* The hoop of a dreamcatcher, usually circular in shape, represents the circle of life. A single bead signifies the spider that wove the web, while multiple beads represent the bad dreams caught in it.

* The feathers hung from dreamcatchers are believed to act as a soft ladder for good dreams to climb their way into the dreamer's mind.

* Sometimes a dreamcatcher includes arrowheads for increased protection and strength, with arrows representing the four corners of the Earth as directed by the wind.

**Dreamcatchers
also appear in some
East Asian cultures
where they are
usually made with
peacock feathers
and placed near
doors and windows.**

Elephant

PLACE OF ORIGIN:
Asia

KEY TRAITS:
Protection, Loyalty, Strength,
Wisdom, Fertility

Sacred in Buddhist and Hindu religions and symbolizing strength, power, stability and wisdom, the elephant is a sign of good luck all over Asia but especially in India and Thailand. The Hindu god Ganesha features the head of an elephant and is thought to bring luck and wisdom, while in Buddhism, the elephant is the guardian of the temples.

Placing an elephant to face your front door brings good luck into the home, and many business owners in Asia will place elephants in the entrance to their shops. The common belief is that the trunk must be up for good luck, and the trunk facing downwards brings bad luck. However, some believe that a trunk facing down allows for good fortune to overcome obstacles and to be passed freely to everyone.

* An elephant figurine facing the main door will protect the house from negative energies or the evil eye. If the elephant statue is facing inside the house, it symbolizes good luck.

* If you are looking for growth in your career, place an elephant in front of the main door to your office to energize your leadership. For more prosperity and success, place the elephant to the north, which is ruled by Kuber, the lord of wealth.

* To stimulate fertility, place a pair of elephants on either side of the door to your bedroom, facing inside. Alternatively, place an elephant statue on each of the bedside tables, facing the bed.

Seven elephants in a
row are considered
especially powerful,
representing
longevity, eternity
and overcoming
death.

Four-leaf Clover

COUNTRY OF ORIGIN:
Ireland

KEY TRAITS:
Love, Luck, Hope, Faith;
Good Fortune, Prosperity

Considered potent good luck symbols in many countries, four-leaf clovers are most closely associated with Ireland – the Emerald Isle. Linked to the country's long Christian history, these clovers resemble the Celtic cross and their four corners are said to represent faith, hope, love and luck.

In fact, legend takes the four-leaf clover back further, tracing it all the way to Adam and Eve, with Eve said to have carried one with her when she and Adam were banished from the Garden of Eden.

Incredibly rare, they are an uncommon variant of the three-leaf clover – the Irish shamrock – and your chances of finding one in the wild are around 1 in 10,000. Little wonder that someone who finds one is bestowed with an abundance of good luck.

* If you are lucky enough to find a four-leaf clover, handle it with care until you can press it between the pages of a book to dry it out.

* If you give your four-leaf clover to another person, it is said you will double your luck.

* Plant a four-leaf clover in your garden to bring luck and prosperity to your home.

* If you're suffering from nightmares, place a four-leaf clover under your pillow for restful sleep and sweet dreams.

According to Celtic folklore, four-leaf clovers help you to see fairies and so avoid their mischief and bad luck.

Gris-gris

COUNTRY OF ORIGIN:
Ghana

KEY TRAITS:
Protection, Love, Luck, Healing

A gris-gris is a small cloth bag containing ritual objects that is worn about the person as a good luck talisman primarily to ward off evil spirits. Gris-gris have their origins in West Africa where they blended Islamic and indigenous African devotions and were shaped according to local beliefs. They developed over time, blending further with voodoo practices when they came to America's southern states with enslaved Africans, but a large element of mystery around them remains.

The bags' specific contents vary regionally and according to their intended purpose, but can include herbs, roots, bones, stones, shells, figurines and a piece of folded paper with prayers, symbols and inscriptions written on it. As well as repelling evil, they are used for healing and to attract love and money.

* The ownership of gris-gris bags has a darker side and they were also used to curse slave masters and bring black magic upon an enemy as part of voodoo and hoodoo practices.

* Gris-gris need to be put together by a specialist practitioner and owners must never open the bag or let others touch it to avoid the risk of its power spilling out.

* To maintain the bag's potency and encourage its help in manifesting your goals, it needs special care; owners are encouraged to play it music, meditate on it and light a weekly incense offering to it.

As recently as the 1980s, gris-gris bags were used as a method of contraception in some West African countries, such as Senegal.

Hamsa

PLACE OF ORIGIN:
Middle East

KEY TRAITS:
Good luck, Protection,
Abundance, Happiness

Dating from ancient times, this hand-shaped amulet wards off the evil eye, protects the wearer from adversity and brings happiness. It is sacred to followers of both the Jewish and Muslim faiths. In the Jewish tradition, it is also known as the "hand of Miriam" and its five fingers symbolize the five books of the Torah and the five senses needed to praise God. In Islamic culture it is also called the "hand of Fatima" and represents the five pillars of Islam. For Hindus and Buddhists, it symbolizes chakras, energy flow in the body, the five senses and the mudras that affect them.

Commonly seen throughout the Middle East and Northern Africa, the hamsa is a symmetrical open palm with three fingers, a thumb on each side and a central eye that sees everything and keeps watch over its owner.

* Often bought as jewellery, in intricate gold or silver filigree, hamsas can be worn or displayed with the fingers pointing up or down. An upward-facing hamsa protects against evil and negativity, while a hamsa facing downwards brings happiness, abundance and fertility to its owner.

* The hamsa is typically worn as a ring or bracelet on the left (receiving) hand. For the amulet to work effectively, focus on positive thoughts and intentions while wearing it.

* The hamsa can also be seen painted on the walls of houses, often in red to echo the ancient practice of using blood from a sacrificed animal. It is also painted or hung above doorways for protection, especially watching over expectant mothers and babies.

Similar to the Western use of the phrase "knock on wood" or "touch wood", a common expression in Israel is "Hamsa, Hamsa, Hamsa, tfu, tfu, tfu", the sound for spitting, supposedly to spit out bad luck.

Horseshoe

PLACE OF ORIGIN:
Western Europe

KEY TRAITS:
Good luck, Protection

Horseshoes have been a much-loved symbol
for luck and protection for over a thousand
years, originally across much of Europe and
more recently in the United States, where
the tales of the Wild West have only boosted
their popularity.

Their luck is said to originate from the actions
of Saint Dunstan, patron saint of blacksmiths,
who tricked the Devil and nailed horseshoes
to his feet, only agreeing to remove them if the
Devil guaranteed never to enter a house with a
horseshoe above the door.

In addition, horseshoes were made of iron,
a magical metal believed by early Europeans
to repel bad fairies and witches. Finally, a
horseshoe traditionally has seven holes, with
the lucky number seven further strengthening
their talismanic qualities.

* There is some debate about whether to hang the horseshoe with ends facing up or down. They are mostly positioned facing up in order to catch and hold all of their luck, not spilling a drop, but some prefer to have them facing down, pouring their luck out over all who pass beneath.

* Horseshoes are thought to be especially lucky if a horse has already worn them.

* In a tradition popularized in Victorian times, brides are given horseshoes on their wedding day, often as a charm to hang from their bouquet. The shoe is then taken to the marital home to bestow its luck and protection on the happy couple.

* It's considered lucky in Ireland to bury a horseshoe under the cornerstone of a newly built house, to bestow good fortune on the people that move into it.

Babe Ruth

According to his coach Eddie Collins, the famous baseball player had a locker "full of charms, fetishes and tokens", which included a miniature totem pole and a wooden horseshoe, engraved with a four-leaf clover, which was fastened to the door.

Jin Chan

COUNTRY OF ORIGIN:
China

KEY TRAITS:
Wealth, Prosperity, Good health, Protection

Jin Chan is a lucky golden toad or bullfrog with three legs that sits on top of a large pile of coins and also carries a coin in its mouth. A popular feng shui charm and also known as the money toad, it fends off misfortune and brings an abundance of luck.

Legend states that this mythical figure – believed to be able to produce gold or silver coins from its mouth – appears near homes or businesses during the full moon, auguring good news, which is usually financial in nature.

Today golden Jin Chan figurines are popularly seen in Chinese homes and businesses, often placed in the wealth or career areas of a building according to feng shui principles.

* Because Jin Chan symbolizes the flow of money, it should always be positioned facing inwards in a house or business, and not towards the door, in order to draw money into the building.

* Keeping a small Jin Chan in your wallet, thus close to you at all times, is another way to work with this lucky talisman. Alternatively, if you are a business owner, place one near the cash register or safe in your place of work, always facing into the room.

* Place the toad in a slightly elevated position on a lower shelf or table to facilitate the best flow of its positive, wealth-related energy.

President Dwight D. Eisenhower

Ike carried three lucky coins in his pocket: an American silver dollar, a British five guinea gold piece and a French franc. It is said he would feel the coins whenever he was trying to make an important decision.

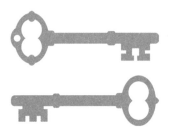

Keys

PLACE OF ORIGIN:
Worldwide

KEY TRAITS:
Fortune, Freedom, Love

One of the oldest good luck charms, keys
are popular amulets the world over. Used in
everyday life to open doors, cupboards and
hidden treasures, they symbolize the unlocking
of barriers and doorways to freedom. In ancient
Greece, key charms were often called the
"keys of life"; holding them overcame spiritual
obstructions and enabled prayers to fly freely
to the gods.

Keys are also associated with the Roman god
Janus – god of beginnings, gates and transitions
– and Portunus, god of keys, doors and ports.
Every August 17th, on Portunus' festival day,
keys were thrown into a fire to summon good
luck for the coming year.

Today, keys are given to offer luck on a 21st
birthday as a young adult opens the door to
their future. They are also shared between
sweethearts as a key to the heart, a token of
exclusive love.

* Having three keys together as a charm is said to bring three-fold luck, as they unlock the doors to health, wealth and love in your life.

* Crossed keys – one silver to denote spiritual authority and one gold for the power of heaven – are a symbol of papal authority in the Catholic Church. They are associated with Saint Peter, who founded the church in Rome and was promised the keys to heaven by Jesus in the Gospel of Matthew.

* Wearing a key on a chain around the neck is said to help you open any physical or spiritual barriers you are experiencing.

* Hang a key upside down on the wall over your bed to prevent bad dreams.

"When good luck knocks at the door, let him in and keep him there. "

Miguel de Cervantes, *Don Quixote*

Ladybird/ Ladybug

PLACE OF ORIGIN:
Western Europe

KEY TRAITS:
Luck, Love, Fertility,
Good weather, Abundance

The name ladybird comes from the Middle Ages when this brightly coloured insect was known as the "beetle of Our Lady", a reference to the Virgin Mary who was often depicted wearing red at the time. Farmers gave them this name in honour of the Virgin, who they credited with sending the bugs to destroy the aphids that attacked their crops.

Farmers have considered it lucky to see a ladybird ever since and this belief soon spread to the rest of society. In Germany they are even called glückskafer, literally "lucky bugs", and seeing one is said to foreshadow good fortune or good news.

Ladybirds also bring luck in the areas of marriage, family and fertility – again linked to their role in protecting crops. A successful harvest meant abundance for the year, which enabled weddings to take place and was seen as a good omen for fertility in marriage.

* If a ladybird lands on you, the number of spots on its back correspond to the number of months of good luck that is headed your way, or the number of months you'll be waiting until your wish comes true.

* Another folk tale states that if a ladybird lands on you and flies away, the next person on which it alights is your true love.

* Catch a ladybird (carefully), make a wish on it and then let it go. Good luck will come from the direction in which it flies away.

* Finding a ladybird in the house indicates luck in money is coming to you. This is believed to link to the insect's role in a successful harvest.

BAD LUCK!

The Black Cat

Although considered auspicious in the East, a black cat walking across your path or walking away from you is believed to be a sign of misfortune and death, a superstition from Medieval times. In folklore, the cat is a spy or courier for witches, able to change into human shape.

BAD LUCK!

Laughing Buddha

COUNTRY OF ORIGIN:
China

KEY TRAITS:
Contentment, Abundance, Happiness,
Prosperity, Wellbeing

This happy figurine of a short man with a pot belly and big smile has spread luck and happiness for hundreds of years. Originating in China, but particularly popular in Thailand, Vietnam and India today, the Laughing Buddha is seen in a range of poses, all of which attract variations of his trademark contentment and prosperity.

Chinese folklore tells of a wandering 10th-century monk known as Budai, who travelled from place to place with a simple cloth sack containing his few possessions. This mystical figure was always cheerful and encouraged people to practise positivity and gratitude in all circumstances. His large belly associated him with abundance and his kind and cheerful demeanour made him especially popular with children.

* A Laughing Buddha carrying a cloth sack signifies the ability to put your troubles and misfortunes in his bag and replace them with positivity and prosperity.

* When depicted with five children at his feet, the Laughing Buddha represents family wellbeing, particularly in relation to children, fertility and good health in general.

* When shown holding beads, the Buddha brings calm and meditative properties, symbolizing wisdom and contentment but also affluence and success.

* A sitting or standing Laughing Buddha shown with gold nuggets or coins represents luck, happiness and wealth. One holding a bowl denotes the good fortune he has gathered to scatter around him.

* If shown with a fan in one hand and a gourd in the other, the Buddha's fan is said to ward off misfortune while the gourd protects health.

Laughing Buddha figures can be seen both in homes and public places, but for his luck to flow he needs to be kept happy – by having his belly rubbed every day.

Lucky Bamboo

COUNTRY OF ORIGIN:
China

KEY TRAITS:
Happiness, Wealth, Longevity

Lucky bamboo is the common name of one of the most popular house plants in the world, the hardy, fast-growing, long-lived *Dracaena*. Known as a good luck symbol for thousands of years throughout Asia, the plant is said to bring happiness, wealth and longevity to the owner if it has three stalks.

Except for the number four, which is usually considered unlucky in Chinese culture, greater numbers of stalks bring additional luck. Five or more stalks will bring you additional good fortune, prosperity, good health, growth, fertility, blessings and completeness. Simply put, as your plant grows and thrives, your health, wealth and happiness will too.

* Give the plant as a gift, especially for someone moving into a new home, to bestow luck, wealth and happiness.

* Place your lucky bamboo in indirect light in the east or south-east of a room to bring luck in the areas of health and wealth. In the office or at work, place the plant in the south-east corner in gentle light to attract prosperity.

* For the most auspicious growing conditions, plant lucky bamboo in a container filled with rocks or pebbles and top it up with filtered or distilled water that should be changed every few weeks.

"The bamboo that bends is stronger than the oak that resists. "

Japanese proverb

Maneki-neko

COUNTRY OF ORIGIN:
Japan

KEY TRAITS:
Success, Good fortune, Prosperity

The maneki-neko waving cat comes from Japan but is now widely seen around the world, especially in Chinatown districts where it's often mistaken for being Chinese. It is beckoning more than waving – in Japanese *maneki* means "to beckon" and *neko* means "cat" – and is a popular talisman for encouraging people to enter shops and restaurants, and for inviting in good luck.

Legend states that a 17th-century ruler took shelter under a tree in a storm when a cat beckoned him to a temple instead. Looking back, he saw the tree struck by lightning, and gave money to the temple in thanks. Its lucky cat was later honoured by the creation of the feline figurines.

Another tale saw a poor shop owner taking in a stray despite having little food of his own. In gratitude, the cat sat at the front of the store, beckoning in customers, and has been a good luck symbol for businesses ever since.

* Maneki-neko should be placed in a busy area, as the cat loves people and wants to be able to see them. This is why they are often seen in a window or entrance to a house or business.

* If the cat's left paw is raised, it is said to bring customers and success to the business and its owners. If the right paw is raised, it is believed to attract wealth.

* The colour of your maneki-neko also holds significance, with white and gold being the most common colours used. White cats are believed to bring happiness in Japanese culture, while gold ones, also known as money cats, bring wealth.

* Blue and green maneki-neko signify academic success, black cats protect against sickness and red cats ward off evil spirits.

Suzanne Farrell

The American ballet dancer was said to take a papier-mâché cat with a missing ear on the road with her for good luck, according to the 1966 *The Ballet Cook Book* by Tanaquil Le Clercq.

Martenitsa

COUNTRY OF ORIGIN:
Bulgaria

KEY TRAITS:
Protection, Luck, Good health

Martenitsa are a pair of small woollen folk dolls from Bulgaria, one red and one white, that are joined together by the same wool they're made from. Named Pizho and Penda, Pizho is the male doll, made predominantly from white wool, while Penda is the female doll of mainly red wool and known by her red skirt.

With their roots in ancient pagan history, they are worn as an amulet during the month of March in order to placate Baba Marta, the mythical old woman who brings the end of winter, and to bring health and blessings while waiting for spring. Martenitsa are worn from March 1st – the Baba Marta Day holiday – until the wearer sees a stork, swallow or tree in blossom, or the end of the month if that is sooner.

* Popular in Bulgaria and neighbouring regions, Martenitsa dolls should be given as gifts to friends and family rather than bought for oneself, and are traditionally worn pinned to clothing or as part of a necklace or bracelet.

* The red wool symbolizes life and birth, while the white wool symbolizes purity. Together they represent the coming of spring and new life, as well as balance and harmony between the male and female, and the constant cycle of life and death.

* Martenitsa dolls must always stay together with the yarn between them remaining unbroken to protect their talismanic properties. When it's time to remove them, they are often tied to a tree to bring it health and good luck in the coming year.

Nénette and
Rintintin are
similar red and
white woollen dolls
found in France,
which were first
seen pinned to the
uniforms of soldiers
as good luck charms
in World War I.

Milagros

COUNTRY OF ORIGIN:
Mexico

KEY TRAITS:
Protection, Religious miracles

Milagros are small religious folk charms popular in Mexico and elsewhere in the southern United States and Latin America. Brought to the New World by the Spanish conquistadores in the 16th century, their roots are in the Catholic practice of offering votives to the saints or to God as part of prayers of supplication or thanks.

Milagros – the Spanish word for miracles – take many forms, including angels and praying figures, sacred hearts, animals, foodstuffs, symbols from the natural world and different parts of the body. Each milagro will have a specific meaning to the person who uses it, which can be literal or figurative. A milagro showing a foot or shoe, for example, might indicate a prayer for a broken bone or for someone going on a journey.

* Milagros are hung with ribbons or pinned to altars, statues or shrines as a sacrificial offering by believers who have made a pilgrimage, in order to give thanks or ask for help from the associated saint.

* They are often made from flattened metal, such as silver, gold, lead or tin, but sometimes also seen carved from wood, bone or wax.

* Milagros can also be carried by people in their pockets as good luck charms or to encourage a general improvement in fortunes related to the specific charm chosen.

" Remember that sometimes not getting what you want is a wonderful stroke of luck. "

Dalai Lama XIV

Nazar

PLACE OF ORIGIN:
Ancient Sumeria, Turkey

KEY TRAITS:
Protection against the evil eye

The evil eye is an envious glare believed in many cultures to bring misfortune to those on receiving end of it. The nazar is a small blue, turquoise and white glass amulet in the form of an unblinking eye, which wards off this malevolent stare and turns its negative energy back on itself.

This is a concept that dates back thousands of years to the Sumerian culture of the Near East. Nazars are blue because this colour represents the sky, the home of the gods where they watch over mortals. Today, they are particularly popular in Turkey, parts of the Balkans, Central Asia and the Middle East, where they are worn as charms or hung in homes for protection.

* Nazar beads or discs are commonly worn as bracelets – by both men and women – but can also be seen on necklaces or earrings. They can be hung from a car's rear-view mirror or from a keychain.

* They are often given at baby showers or to newborns, who can be particularly at risk from the jealousy of the evil eye as they are precious gifts bestowed to family. It is customary to hide a nazar in a baby's clothing for hidden protection.

* Cleanse your nazar when you first have it or if you feel it has soaked up a lot of negative energy. Some people prefer to wash the nazar in fresh water from a stream, saltwater or holy water, or bathe it in sunlight or moonlight.

"A deep man believes the evil eye can wither, the heart's blessing can heal and that love can overcome all odds. "

Ralph Waldo Emerson,
"The Conduct of Life"

Omamori

COUNTRY OF ORIGIN:
Japan

KEY TRAITS:
Blessings and protection,
often with a specific focus

Sold in Japanese Buddhist temples and Shinto shrines, omamori are small silk brocade pouches containing prayers to different deities and religious figures. These charming amulets are sanctified at the religious site and often given as gifts from one person to another to wish them well and bestow protection and good luck.

Omamori first became popular around 400 years ago in Japan's Edo period and the prayers they contain used to be written on wood. Now usually inscribed on tiny pieces of paper, they cover a range of popular topics. These include invoking wealth and happiness or warding off evil, as well as success in the areas of love, education, health, fertility and beauty. The prayers can be general or incredibly specific and devotees choose them with great care.

* Keep your omamori about your person –
perhaps attached to a bag or purse – and never
open the pouch or its luck will escape.

* Don't worry if the pouch becomes a little
scruffy as wear and tear is a good sign that
the amulet is doing its job of protecting you.

* Omamori should be replaced annually, on or
soon after the New Year, to get rid of any bad
luck from the previous year. Ideally, return them
to their place of purchase where they are burned
as a sign of respect to the deity that protected
their owner during the year.

BAD LUCK!

Gifting Clocks

In the East, many believe that gifting a clock is an omen of an early death. Clocks, associated with the ticking of time, can symbolize the end of one's journey, and the phrase "giving a clock" sounds similar to "sending someone on their last journey" in Cantonese.

BAD LUCK!

Pig

COUNTRY OF ORIGIN:
Germany

KEY TRAITS:
Good luck, Wealth, Fertility

Pigs have been a symbol of luck and prosperity in Germanic areas since ancient times when Roman historians wrote of tribes who carried images of wild boar as mascots for protection in battle. In the Middle Ages, owning a pig signified affluence and an ability to eat meat when so many had none, and pigs were even given a high worth in medieval board games, further cementing their reputation.

Today, glücksschwein, meaning "lucky pig", is a popular token of affluence and fertility in Germany and Austria, and the German expression *Schwein haben* – literally, "to have a pig" – means you've been blessed with good fortune. The pig's association with wealth has crossed over into many cultures, such as with piggy bank money boxes, in which children save their pennies.

* Glücksschwein often feature on good luck cards or are given as gifts around New Year in Germany and Austria. These might be small figurines, painted enamel charms or, most popularly, marzipan sweets.

* They are often combined with a four-leaf clover and sometimes also a chimney sweep, in a charming combination of good luck symbols that only adds to their strength.

* In China, the pig is seen as one of the most auspicious zodiac signs and is the sign associated with wealth.

* There is a Swiss tradition of presenting a piglet to the bride and groom on their wedding day to bestow luck and fertility on the happy couple.

Lucky pig charms for charm bracelets were popular in the late 19th century and early 20th century, often made of silver or gold. Expressions such as "happy as a pig in the mire", "a pig in clover" and "you lucky pig" reflect the pig's associations with happiness, wealth and good luck.

Pysanky

COUNTRY OF ORIGIN:
Ukraine

KEY TRAITS:
Strength, Health, Love, Wealth,
Fertility, Protection

A popular Easter tradition in Ukraine and other Eastern European countries, pysanky are intricately decorated, hand-painted and dyed eggs made during Holy Week to celebrate this Christian festival and its symbolic message of rebirth.

The smoothest, most perfectly shaped eggs are collected during Lent (the period running up to Easter), their insides are removed and they are decorated with different colours and patterns to make pysanky. Particular designs and colour combinations are passed down through families but often feature elaborate geometric or floral patterns, created with special styluses and using plant dyes and wax-resist methods. One of the most universal patterns used is the triangle, which represents the Holy Trinity.

Pysanky are then given a special blessing at church on Easter Sunday, after which they are seen as sacred, talismanic objects, and then they are given to children, family and friends as a symbolic gift of new life.

* After the Easter holiday is over, place a pysanka in each corner of your home to watch over it and bring good luck for the coming year.

* Choose a pysanka decorated with ornate spiral designs as, according to Ukrainian lore, these are especially protective as they trap devils and other evil spirits within their spirals.

* Bury crushed pysanky shells in your vegetable garden to encourage a bumper harvest or add them to cattle feed to nurture strong and healthy animals.

Pysanky were
ideally made from
the first-laid eggs
of young hens.
These needed to be
fertilized eggs to
ensure fertility in
the home.

Rabbit's Foot

COUNTRY OF ORIGIN:
Worldwide

KEY TRAITS:
Good luck, Protection against
evil and disease, Fertility

Keeping a rabbit's hind foot has been considered protective and lucky since ancient times when Roman author Pliny the Elder claimed that carrying a hare's foot cured gout. From the 1500s to 1800s, they were a popular amulet carried by Europeans for protection against disease, and have only increased in popularity since then.

Associated with luck, fertility, renewal and spring in most corners of the globe, the rabbit's foot charm is perhaps most closely connected to the American South, where some believed rabbits were shapeshifters; a rabbit's foot may have once been a witch's foot, or worse. Possessing such a thing neutralizes the evil threat, making it an especially powerful talisman for warding off evil. And if the foot was the back left and the rabbit was captured in a cemetery, under a new or full moon on a Friday – better still; if Friday 13th, its potency dramatically increased.

* Celtic tradition describes how rabbits (who live underground) can speak to the spirits of the underworld and they were revered as a result.

* It's customary in the British Isles and United States for "rabbits" or "white rabbit" to be the first thing you say on the first day of a new month to bring you luck for the whole month.

* Keep your rabbit's foot in a pocket, wallet or handbag, attach it to a keychain or wear it as jewellery. Set your intention for the luck you wish to attract, as focusing on visualizing good fortune increases the effectiveness of the charm.

Ernest Hemingway

As the writer recounts in *The Moveable Feast*, while living in Paris in 1921–8, Hemingway carried a horse chestnut and a rabbit's foot in his right pocket for good luck. He wrote, "The fur had been worn off the rabbit's foot long ago . . . the claws scratched in the lining of your pocket and you knew your luck was still there."

Scarab Beetle

COUNTRY OF ORIGIN:
Egypt

KEY TRAITS:
Rebirth, Resurrection,
Transformation, Protection

The scarab beetle as a good luck charm dates to 2345 BCE and is associated with Khepri, the Egyptian god of the rising sun and creation. Because the scarab rolls dung across the ground, the Egyptians associated it with the sun's journey across the sky, and thus the cycle of life. The scarab would also lay its eggs in the bodies of dead animals, connecting it with life recreated from death.

Often depicted in art and used as amulets, the scarab symbolized protection and good fortune. The beetles were also frequently used as seals for important documents, denoting the owner's power and authority. They were placed in tombs, over the heart of the deceased, to ensure safe passage to the afterlife.

* Wear scarab jewellery to protect against evil forces. Victorian jewellers used enamel, glass and semi-precious gemstones, in art deco and art nouveau scarab designs.

* Choose an amulet according to the colours of the scarab beetle: red represents the sun god Ra; yellow, the sun and the desert; blue, the Nile; and green, growth.

* A winged scarab is a symbol of an easy and peaceful transformation and rebirth, so particularly powerful when you are embarking on a life change, such as a change of home or career, a relationship transition or a death in the family.

The Scarab of Hatshepsut, a large, ornate scarab beetle made of gold and decorated with precious stones, is believed to have belonged to one of the most powerful female pharaohs.

Torito de Pucará

COUNTRY OF ORIGIN:
Peru

KEY TRAITS:
Protection, Happiness,
Fertility, Equilibrium

The Andean town of Pucará in southern Peru is named for the pre-Hispanic Pucará civilization, which flourished for almost 2,000 years and was known for its pyramidal architecture and ceramic art. The distinctive ceramic bulls – toritos de Pucará – seen in the region today are a blend of this culture with the ideas and animals introduced by the Spanish conquistadores in the 1500s.

These colourful figures depict the bulls that appeared in Spanish festivals, often splashed with paint and driven half mad by having spices rubbed on their nose. This is why toritos are always shown with wild staring eyes and the tongue out, licking their nose. They represent strength and fertility and are usually displayed in pairs, hung above doors or standing on rooftops, to protect and bring happiness to the home. A pair of toritos also symbolizes the duality of the universe and the blending of positive and negative energies to reach balance.

* The highly stylized design of the bulls holds significance – the small handle on its saddle represents strength in marriage while the hole at the handle's base symbolizes fertility.

* The colourful decoration of toritos also has meaning, with spiral designs echoing a karmic belief in the circular nature of existence where one's actions, good and bad, will similarly affect one's future luck.

* In the Pucará region, it is not uncommon to see two bulls on a roof with a cross in between in a fusion of Andean and Christian cultures, each further strengthening the other's protective qualities.

"Luck must be dealt with like health: enjoy it when it is good, be patient when it is bad. "

François de La Rochefoucauld,
Reflections; or Sentences and Moral Maxims

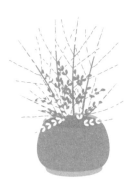

White Heather

COUNTRY OF ORIGIN:
Scotland

KEY TRAITS:
Luck in love and marriage;
Protection against evil, hunger and fire

Hills and glens covered in heather have been
a national symbol of Scotland for hundreds of
years. Further back still, heather was sacred
to the druids and associated with the magical
summer solstice. While it is usually purple,
there is a rare white variety and it's considered
extremely lucky to find some, rather like finding
a four-leaf clover in neighbouring Ireland.

White heather is best known for bringing luck
in love and marriage, a quality that comes from
the tale of Malvina, a young maiden betrothed to
a Celtic warrior who died in battle. He sent her a
bouquet of purple heather as a final token of his
love and when she received it her tears turned
the purple flowers white. This miracle prompted
her to declare that white heather would from
that day bring good fortune to those who find it.

* One Scottish legend says that white heather only grows on land where no blood has been spilled in battle – rare in a country with a warring history – while another says that it marks the graves of fairies.

* White heather is believed to have protective qualities and was hung in Highland homes long ago to guard against evil, fire and hunger.

* The popularity of white heather as a lucky charm, and the fashion for it to appear in bridal bouquets, spread from Scotland to the whole of the UK after Queen Victoria was given some by a servant who spied it on moorland and ran to collect it for her to pass on its luck.

Said to be a favourite of
Robert Burns, a herbal
infusion of heather
tops was used to soothe
nerves and to treat
coughs, arthritis
and rheumatism in the
Scottish Highlands.

Wishbone

PLACE OF ORIGIN:
Ancient Etruria

KEY TRAITS:
Luck, Divination, Granting of wishes

Superstitions surrounding the wishbone
date back as far as 700 BCE when the ancient
Etruscans believed birds were oracles who
could foretell the future. They left the Y-shaped
furcula bone out to dry before using it as a
divination tool and people would stroke it for
luck and make wishes. The Romans continued
this practice and it spread through Europe
where, in the Middle Ages, the wishbones of
geese eaten on feast days were used to predict
the weather.

From the 17th century onwards, the practice of
pulling the wishbone after eating a large bird
became common, whereby two people would
hold one side each with a little finger and pull
on it until it broke. The person left holding the
larger piece then made a wish; if the bone broke
evenly, both parties got a wish.

* Wishbones were known as "merrythoughts" in England during the 17th and 18th centuries.

* The Medieval Teutonic Knights were said to consult wishbones before going into battle, changing their plans according to what the bones divined.

* As the person breaking off the larger half of the wishbone is the one who gets to wish, some have suggested that the wishbone-pulling tradition gave rise to the phrases "lucky break" and "bad break".

Upside-down Chopsticks

In Japanese and Chinese culture, placing chopsticks straight up in a bowl of rice is taboo, as it is reminiscent of the food offerings left for the dead. At traditional funerals, a bowl of rice with upright chopsticks is a way to honour the deceased and their ancestors.

Worry Dolls

COUNTRY OF ORIGIN:
Guatemala

KEY TRAITS:
Aids sleep, Relieves troubles

Guatemalan worry dolls are tiny handmade dolls constructed from wire, wool and textiles and shown in traditional Mayan dress. Particularly popular with children, they act as a good luck charm to help those with anxiety get a good night's sleep. Some traditions state you need one doll for each worry, while others say you need a group of six so you have one doll for each day of the week apart from Sunday, which is a rest day for them.

The origin story of the dolls describes how there was once a Mayan princess named Ixmucane who was as kind as she was beautiful. The sun god offered her any gift she would like and she chose something that would take away all human worries and cares. Worry dolls represent this gift – they will listen to your worries and make them disappear while you sleep.

* Hold a worry doll and tell it your troubles before going to sleep. After sharing a worry with each of your dolls, place them under your pillow so they can do their work while you sleep. In the morning, retrieve your dolls and keep them in a little box or cloth pouch so they can recharge for the next evening.

Wheel of Fortune

8 ways to make your own luck every day

- Set Clear Goals
- Jump On Opportunities
- Follow Your Gut Instinct
- Surround Yourself with Friends & Mentors
- Expect Good Things to Happen
- Visualize Success
- Be Proactive
- Identify Your Fears & Face Them